A Christian Contemplation on Creation

Proverbs and Poems

Dr Ali Ansarifar

Copyright© Dr Ali Ansarifar 2025

All rights reserved. No part of this book may be reproduced in any form by photocopying, electronic, or mechanical means—including information storage or retrieval systems—without written permission from both the copyright owner and the publisher.

The right of Dr Ali Ansarifar to be identified as the author of this work has been asserted by him in accordance with the Copyright, Designs, and Patents Act 1988 and any subsequent amendments thereto.

A catalogue record for this book is available from the British Library.

All Scripture quotations have been taken from the Good News Bible, Today's English, The Bible Societies, Collins/Fontana versions of the Bible

ISBN: 978-1-916801-57-8

1st Edition 2025 by Kingdom Publishers, London, UK.

You can purchase copies of this book from any leading bookstore or at: **www.kingdompublishers.co.uk**

Dedication

I dedicate this book to hard working Christians and the long-suffering humanity.

Contents

Preface	9
Chapter 1 - The Lord God and his creation	11
Chapter 2 - The universe and humanity	16
Chapter 3 - Jesus Christ and salvation	24
A poetic reflection on life	31
References	33
About the author	34
About the book	35
A personal reflection	36
Final remarks by the author	44
Books by the author	45

Preface

When Jesus meets a person on a journey to Damascus, the person's life will never be the same. A Christian journey to find the truth is an experience of learning that is unique in all its aspects and content. Jesus Christ is the central figure, and the truth that he reveals changes one's perspective and understanding of God, humanity, and the world forever. What is the best way to communicate this Christocentric reality to others without compromising the individual's experience in which the reality has been revealed?

This personal dimension validates the truth and confirms the biblical narrative. The revealed truth must always remain inside a person's experience of life and address the concerns and living conditions of others to have any meaning and credibility. A Christian reflection on creation that consists of proverbs and poems provides a less formal and a more engaging setting for dialogue and discussion about this subject. We must remain steadfast in hope for a better future for humanity, with Jesus Christ remaining the focus of our attention and devotion. One way to express our devotion and faith is through poetry and the use of proverbs.

Chapter 1 - The Lord God and his creation

1. The entirety emerged to redeem the duality of light and darkness. The light will leave the place where it came into existence of its own accord and coexisted with darkness and go to a new place where it will be oneness in the form of the fatherhood of mankind and then rests. In this light, the beginning was, and the ending will be. We come from the duality of light and darkness, and we will go to the oneness of the light. In Jesus Christ, the entirety rests, and the duality will be changed into a perfect unity where eternity begins.

2. The deep state has emerged due to the angelic rebellion in heaven. The primary objective of God's salvation plan is to defeat the deep state, even if it means giving up humanity to the violent impulses of history.

3. Light has constructive qualities such as creativity, decency, compassion, forgiveness, healing, wisdom, and a good life. There is destructiveness, hatred, lies, confusion, dishonesty, ignorance, and death in the darkness. It is puzzling why so many humans choose darkness over light. Then again, light knows his children, and darkness knows hers.

4. It is a fantasy to think that God created the world with love. Rather, it is more likely that the world was made for love to flourish. There is so little precious love in the hearts of men. So much investment has been made for so little yield.

5. It's a common mistake for humans to believe in a personal god. When did God ever say to a person, 'I love you.'? Should we not

love God? If we can't love our neighbour, how can we love God?

6. Imagine a universe that is quiet, cold, dark, and lifeless for perpetuity. There are no cries, no suffering, no bloodshed, no injustices, no lies, no hypocrisies, and no unfulfilled promises and false hope. Knowing the origin of things helps one to understand their dire states.

7. A farmer sows wheat seeds into the ground. As the wheat grows, weeds appear and overtake it. The farmer wonders about the origin of the weeds but is unable to prevent them from harming the wheat. What is the origin of the weeds?

8. A farmer harvests his grains of wheat and makes them into flour. He gives the flour to a baker who mixes it with water to make a dough. The baker then uses the dough to make a loaf of bread and alms it to the hungry. The hungry eat the bread and say, "Blessed is the baker who made the bread, and hallowed be the farmer who sowed the wheat, for he knew of my hunger."

9. A farmer planted wheat seeds in his farm and watered the soil until wheat grew. But, to his bitter disappointment, the harvest produced little wheat and many weeds. How sad that so much farmland is squandered for the sake of a few grains of wheat.

10. The seed was good, but the soil was infertile and the harvest poor. How can the harvest be blamed for the soil's infertility and the sower's mentality?

11. Mankind carries the burden of the light's redemption on its shoulders and what a heavy burden it is to bear. The faithful are holy ground on which the light stands and shines through for

others to see.

12. God created Adam and Eve with His virtues. Adam and Eve procreated mankind by lust and disobedience to God's Command not to procreate. One wonders why the Holy God has so much mercy on the Children of Sin.

13. The children of Adam and Eve pursue injustice, violence, and bloodshed. Children are inheritors of their parents. It's a shame that our parents were so ungodly, and we must suffer the consequences.

14. The story of ancient Israel is like this. A farmer planted a seed in the ground. The seed grew into a tree, but the tree produced no fruit. When the seed died, the die was cast, and the farmer had no say.

15. It is truly amazing that the fate of mankind has been shaped by a covenant with the Holy God which had no get-out clause and no chance of succeeding. But, for those who seek the Lord God in earnest, in Jesus Christ the eternal truth dwells. When they seek, they shall find and upon finding, they will be disturbed, and being disturbed, they will be bewildered. This is a story like no other.

16. Neither the Holy God nor ancient Israel ever planned for a Messianic figure or temple-worship . While God saw the salvation of Israel in the purification of its inner heart, Israel believed its salvation was in the destruction of its mortal enemies. God's anointed Saviour, Jesus Christ, cleanses the heart, but what benefit does it have for Israel, which faces destruction by its gentile enemies?

17. Humans like to thank God for the gift of life, if only they had the chance to overcome despair, anxiety, insecurity, and confusion. It is a pity that most of us can never do that.

18. God loves you, and Jesus loves you. What a strange love that does not save us from ourselves.

19. Why does God need to be prayed and praised by angels and humans? It is truly amazing that humans offer their genuine devotion to God despite assaults on their dignity and innocence. Are we not more precious than the angels in heaven?

20. An examination of biblical history asserts that God is impersonal. But human wisdom denies this assertion and resorts to old fables. Where is the truth?

21. When dualism prevented God from redeeming humankind by building a model nation through a covenant with ancient Israel, He resorted to monism to save His people. In Jesus Christ, dualism was dissolved and replaced by monism. The sick were healed, the dead were resurrected, and the sinners were forgiven. Monism saves the soul, and God's mercy takes us to it. Salvation cannot be achieved through any religion, religious belief, dogmatic ideas, or ritual.

22. The race to Jerusalem began when God separated light from darkness. Who would arrive in Jerusalem first? Light or darkness? The race has been won by darkness. What is the future of Jerusalem?

23. For some people, life is a journey of despair, unhappiness, failure, and rejection, and for others, it is a journey of fulfilment, happiness, security, and acceptance. Is not life a lottery? Who is drawing the numbers?

24. Since all things have been made for the glory of God, we may pray for his kingdom to come and his will to be done on Earth as it is in heaven. Prayers for earthly things are foolishness to the Lord.

Chapter 2 - The universe and humanity

25. It is a wonder of all wonders that righteousness comes into existence from mortal flesh despite such immense darkness and adversity. For a mortal, righteousness is the path to salvation and eternal life.

26. Humans have as much choice in their conception in the womb as God has certainty in creating beings who will remain perfect with no deficiencies in them. How can mankind be responsible for its sinful deeds and suffer the ensuing punishment if at its creation deficiencies corrupted its constitution and its soul?

27. A soul who is formed from a fertile dust bears fruit and is blessed, but a soul who is formed from an infertile dust bears no fruit and is cursed. No man can choose the dust which forms him; then how can mankind have free will if it has never had free choice?

28. When we strip away the worthless knowledge and wisdom that the world has given us and trash it without fear, we will then become the children of the living God and receive the truth.

29. The human soul is like soil. It never produces exactly what is expected when it is planted, but one must make do with the harvest it yields, as little as it may be.

30. Blessed are those whose inner hearts seek God the Father. For their sakes, the truth was revealed in Jesus Christ.

31. Every man is like farmland. When the land is inspected, the farmer says, "How disappointing that the harvest is so poor. If

only I had a say when the land was formed."

32. Take Jehovah as your Lord and follow His moral law or love the world and walk through the valley of death as ancient Israel did.

33. As was the case with Abraham, the yearning for God comes from the heart. So, let this be the prayer of the righteous.

34. Human wisdom searches for the truth diligently. How can mortality, ignorance and vanity find the truth which has been sealed securely in the beauty and mystery of eternity for a few to know who take the Yoke of Christ and serve the Holy God for the redemption of mankind?

35. Since mankind's natural religious instincts are to worship pagan gods and offer blood sacrifices in temples dedicated to idols, one wonders why the Holy God commanded a large group of people to put their trust in him solely and obey His moral laws unreservedly. How can enforced monotheism and the command to follow rigid external moral laws remedy ignorance, ungodliness, apathy, and vanity in the hearts of sinful men?

36. A biblical understanding of the history of the Jewish people helps us to know the story of mankind in its entirety. It is a wonder of all wonders that the fate of such a small nation has shaped the destiny of all nations.

37. We do not know how the final act will unfold on the stage of human history, but we may speculate that the Catholic Church, the Third Temple in Jerusalem, the anti-Christ, and the Islamic invasion of the Holy Land will have a decisive impact on the coming events and the closing of the age.

38. Humanity is a failed enterprise that is run by the worst sinners and funded by the most corrupt Ponzi schemes in the world. It's foolish to believe in human progress and trust the world. Where can one find hope for the future?

39. The dead and the living are citizens of the vanity fair. What difference does it make if one is dead or alive? It is best not to have been born at all.

40. When facing the judgement seat of Christ, say, "No Comment." A person who has had no say in his/her own existence cannot be condemned.

41. Today is the day of judgement, and tomorrow is when the sentence is passed. Relish the moment before the citizenship of hell arrives.

42. God loves you and Jesus loves you, but your neighbour hates you. Why hate one's neighbours, whom we can see and praise and worship the God whom we do not see? God is never here, but our neighbour is always nearby.

43. "You must follow the rules in the Vanity Fair." The rules are made to deceive us.

44. The order of the day is vanity, vanity, and vanity. Enjoy the show for now because the truth will trouble you greatly.

45. All things come from darkness and shall return to it. For now, delight in the little light there is. Darkness is waiting in the wings.

46. Men engage in deception, lying, hurting, harming, theft, betrayal,

and murder. It is no wonder why the light in the world is so dim.

47. There are two types of people in the Vanity Fair. Those who accept all the lies they are told, while those who remain sane. How long can their sanity endure?

48. Why seek the truth that will trouble you? Believe in fairy tales and be happy.

49. Darkness always prevails. Search for the little light there is, and it will save you.

50. Trust all the lies you're told about God and you will be deceiving yourself.

51. Life is like walking through a field full of thorns. One must constantly watch to avoid getting injured. By the time one reaches the opposite side of the field, it will be too late to appreciate the day. Why bother going through the field at all?

52. Sing, dance, pray, and praise whilst you have the opportunity, as the alternative is too terrible to even think about.

53. How can humans keep their sanity in a world that is full of injustice, lies, hate, violence, wars, and bloodshed? By saying: "I am here to share the burden. What a privilege."

54. It's remarkable how many individuals discover the truth during their solitude. However, solitude is not the norm.

55. We are on a journey towards our destination. It is a pity that there are so many potholes on the way. Sadly, some of us will not make it.

56. The kingdoms of God and hell are among us. How many people will make the right choice? Perhaps the choice has already been made and we are moving forward.

57. All roads lead to Damascus in this world. Look what happened to Damascus.

58. So many people travel to nowhere in a frenzy, and when they arrive at their unintended destinations, they wish they were somewhere else. The scheme of providence does not allow for return journeys. Those who are met on their way to nowhere by a Samaritan are likely.

59. When you see orphans, poor, broken-hearted, rejected, betrayed, and downhearted, shed a tear or two. This is humility gone mad.

60. It is strange that we are born into this world without our consent, set on a journey which we never planned, arrive at destinations which we never intended, and leave the world at a time which we never choose. We are expected to be grateful for the gift of life. Imagine if we had all the choices we desired. How much more gratitude would we have shown?

61. Do not worry too much about your fate. It is all done for the glory of God, and you may not even be included in his scheme. Enjoy life because you do not know what is waiting for you ahead.

62. Among the human virtues such as compassion, integrity, faith, loyalty, innocence, charity, and honesty, innocence is by far the greatest asset of all. It is unforgivable to actively harm innocence.

63. Courage is a human virtue. Those who question the given narratives and assumptions about God are the bravest of all men. Those who do not, are the most religious and, by nature, timid.

64. What is the greatest quality in human nature? Is it love? Where there is love, the opposite, hate must also be. There is a high price to pay for the noblest achievement of human nature.

65. The idea that humans can influence and shape the processes in history and the unfolding events is foolish. History is reaching a conclusion that was created by the events of the dawn of time.

66. The welcome party of Satan on Earth is ungodliness, inhumanity, lawlessness, cruelty, hate, lies, bloodshed, immorality, and denial. Everything is ready for the master of darkness to arrive.

67. Human relationships with gods in pre-Abrahamic religions were based on fear, ignorance, superstition, and blood sacrifices. The Abrahamic religions are linked to the Crusades, antisemitism, and Jihad. Where is godliness?

68, The universe is full of mysteries and marvels. But one stands out above all. It is a wonder of all wonders that humans still believe in God, praise, and glorify His name despite all the evidence suggesting that their faith and goodwill have no impact on their immediate conditions or the predicament they are in. The Lord God's relationship with humanity is marked by this greatest mystery.

69. Humans are often reminded of their sinful nature, shortcomings, and the need to beg for mercy and forgiveness from God. But they are never told why they should feel guilty and shameful for their actions if they have never had a say in their conception and

constitution. Where is justice in all this?

70. There is a saying that patience is a virtue. Faith in the Lord God amidst darkness is a virtue too. The faithful are so immersed in their daily struggles that they no longer realise how noble and precious they are in the sight of God, despite all their failures.

71. Life without faith is a great gift that is wasted, and faith without patience is void.

72. What will the universe gain if human dignity, innocence, sensitivity, and life are destroyed so ruthlessly? These noble features were intended to be cherished and safeguarded. Why aren't they?

73. Faithful people pray, fast, mourn, and give alms. In the event of a disaster, none of these will help them.

74. If every man could make a wish, what would it be? Some may wish they never lived, some may wish for a better life here and now. The majority may wish they had free will. Regrettably, the human heart is denied what it truly desires.

75. Rigid and abstract religious belief hinders man's relationship with God. A faith that does not sympathise with the long-suffering humanity and hides behind man-made religions and meaningless rituals bears no fruit.

76. It is amazing that the salvation of the righteous is secured by the sinful deeds of others. Righteousness shines when it is battered by the actions of the unrighteous. How else can the Lord God separate the sheep from the goats?

77. Those who inflict pain, suffering, and death on the defenceless and innocent are granted a day in this life. What is a day in the scheme of eternity?

78. Trust in the wisdom and promises of mortal men and be damned. Trust in the word of God and inherit eternal life.

79. When light shines in darkness, it brings hope. When darkness obscures the light, it brings fear. Keep gazing at the light, and fear will run away.

80. Love is constructive and spontaneous, and hate is destructive and divisive. Be spontaneous and see God.

81. There is a planned destiny for every believer in the scheme of God's providence. But so many are walking in a maze which goes around and around and around and has no purpose. Will they ever get tired of their futile journey?

82. It is lethal to play with the power of darkness. It is even worse when sin comes into the mix. Humans have the worst of both worlds. Luckily, death frees us from both.

83. Imagine you are in a room that is pitch black. Does it matter how big or small the room is? Now imagine you are in a bright room. The light defines the size of the room and shows its limits. When love is at play, all the dimensions disappear, and the universe becomes boundless. Love is more precious than light.

Chapter 3 - Jesus Christ and salvation

84. The Disciples said to Jesus, "Tell us how our end will come to pass." Jesus said, "Then have you laid bare the beginning, so that you are seeking the end? For the end will be where the beginning is. Blessed is the person who stands at rest in the beginning. And that person will be acquainted with the end and will not taste death." [1] (Thomas 18) So, let us visit the beginning, where it all happened.

85. The Holy God sowed a redeemer in the womb of the Virgin Mary. The redeemer became incarnate in Jesus Christ, healed the sick, consoled the bereaved, forgave sinners, raised hope for the oppressed, converted the pagan, and resurrected the dead. The righteous cry, "Blessed is the womb that gave birth to my redeemer, and hallowed be the Father who bestows mercy and rest on my soul."

86. Duality arose when light emerged of its own accord from darkness. And from the duality came the world's struggle. It is only in the person of Jesus Christ that duality is nullified, and perfect oneness is achieved. Happy are those who make the journey to Christ and leave behind the destruction and mayhem of this world to find rest for their souls.

87. We come from the hell of mass extinctions, natural disasters, asteroid impacts, epidemics of disease, famine, injustice, and tribal, regional, and global warfare and bloodshed, and we are going to the hell of judgement and damnation. But, how wise are those who trust Jesus Christ to get them out of this mayhem and

darkness and bring them to the light of the Father.

88. The truth is revealed to the meek and righteous without theatrics. It is at the heart of the coming deception to hypnotise the senses and seduce humans into believing lies and acting ungodly. What a terrible fate awaits those who will be deceived!

89. Man's biggest folly is to think that the truth can be found in religion and religious rituals. How can religious dogmas and belief systems fathom a love which seeks, finds, heals, enlightens, and resurrects one to wholeness in Jesus Christ?

90. To deceive and enslave humans, the forces of evil and their principalities wrapped the biblical truth in lies, pretends, claims, and counterclaims and presented it to the world as the truth. It is in Jesus Christ that this deception is unmasked, the truth is revealed, and the righteous man is freed from its clutches.

91. When I survey the wonderous Cross, I see centuries of invasion, conquest, subjugation, oppression, persecution, injustice, division, immoral acquisition of people's land and wealth, discrimination, betrayal, slavery and bloodshed. I see a collective punishment of all mankind for abandoning the Lord God's moral law and rejecting Jesus Christ the Saviour. But also I see hope of forgiveness, redemption and eternal life. I see a kingdom of justice, peace, immense Joy and abundant love promised to those who take the Yoke of Christ and follow him for the glory of God and service to mankind. I see a promise living within fulfilled and righteousness prevailed for perpetuity.

92. There is peace and fulfilment in the oneness of Jesus Christ. And there is confusion and damnation in the duality of things. God's mercy reaches those who choose to leave the duality of the

world behind through repentance and seek salvation in Jesus Christ. It is the longing of the inner heart for the divine that frees a mortal from the clutches of duality, and when the inner heart is coupled with God's moral law, perfect unity is achieved, like in Jesus Christ.

93. Jesus never goes to those who wait for him. He comes to those who strive to be like him.

94. You can never find God in the dark places. Take the light of Christ, and God will shine like a star.

95. It is incredible that flesh comes into being from the light and inhabits material poverty. It is also remarkable that flesh has an inner heart that seeks after its Creator, the light. It is even more astounding that Jesus Christ redeems the inner soul of mortal man, changing it into pure light for perpetuity.

96. A call to share the gospel with others is a privilege granted to a few who are called to serve Jesus Christ for the glory of God and redemption of humanity.

97. A perfect being can never be created instantly since a being comes into existence of its own accord. And when it does, it can thenceforth be made perfect like Jesus Christ by the Holy God.

98. Anybody who finds the truth in the Bible wonders why human beings' innocence, self-worth, dignity, and self-respect are violated so belligerently for so long. By God's grace and mercy, all that is noble and righteous in human nature will be changed into a perfect oneness in Jesus Christ for eternity. But first, repentance must come.

99. Redemption rests with the Cross, and damnation is with the sword. Whoever has mercy through the Cross will live despite the sword. But whoever has no hope in the Cross will perish by the sword.

100. "Crucify him," the crowd shouted. The Cross of Calvary became a sword of destruction for all. For those in the east, the west, the north, and the south, the sword brought immense suffering and death. Reprisal is falling on the sword-bearer, and one wonders for whom the bell is tolling.

101. As it was with Moses, Jesus was the holy ground on which God stood and revealed Himself to humankind. But when God relinquished the holy ground, Jesus cried, "Father, why have you forsaken me?" Why did God forsake Jesus on the cross?

102. The faithful's inner hearts yearn for God, but they struggle with the keeping of the moral law and commit sins, alienating them from God. God removed alienation by writing His moral law on Jesus' heart, who had faith like Abraham, and produced a perfect being who is freed from the clutches of destructive duality for all time. Now all the faithful can be made perfect like Jesus Christ and inherit eternal life.

103. Death nullifies humans, and only God's grace can resurrect us in Christ. Death did not nullify Jesus, who was resurrected before he went on the cross. Since death has no intrinsic element of resurrection, it is a fantasy to expect resurrection to eternal life outside of Christ.

104. All humans arrive at the point of death. Those who are in Christ pass through it, as Jesus has done, and those who are in the world will perish into the void of darkness when the duality

dissolves. Only the good will escape the destructive clutches of duality.

105. The great deception claims that an ostentatious temple, eye-catching religious rituals, and needless blood sacrifices are godly and lead to salvation. It is in denial of God and salvation in Jesus Christ.

106. There have been speculations and disputes about the identity of Jesus Christ. It is claimed that Jesus was a Jew. However, this cannot be so since Judaism could never have produced a Messiah who preached submission to the will of Rome. Jewish history demanded that a Messiah wage war against the might of Rome to liberate the Jews from servitude and oppression. This is not a universal Messiah.

107. Duality in human nature is made of: good; faith; honesty; courage; care; love; compassion; mercy; generosity; sharing; forgiveness; justice; integrity; self-control; and prudence. And bad is made of: hate; indifference; greed; dishonesty; cruelty; harm; injustice; arrogance; delusion; envy; selfishness; ego; lies; and murder. Salvation is in Jesus Christ, in whom all that is good is incarnate. So, in him who is the bridal chamber, the soul rests, and the truth and mystery of the universe are revealed.

108. Jesus is here, Jesus is there, and Jesus is everywhere. For the blinds, Jesus is nowhere to be seen.

109. Jesus Christ will greet the righteous in the bridal chamber. The unjust have already been in the chamber of their own indignation, but they don't yet realise it.

110. How has humanity managed to endure centuries of insecurity, uncertainty, suffering, war, and bloodshed? By creating and believing in stories that are based on fantasies, wishful thinking, misguided wisdom, and mythology, rather than the truth. Jesus has the truth.

111. There is a truth in the Bible that is secure in Jesus Christ, and only a few will discover it, with God's permission. It transcends God, humans, and the universe itself. Knowing that it will transform the faith of an individual.

112. Darkness hides all our iniquities. Come to the light of Christ and be redeemed.

113. Do not be ashamed of who you are and what you are. It is for your sake that Jesus preached the Sermon on the Mount.

114. We are all walking blindly in the dark until crashing into a brick wall. It never is too late to ask Jesus to light the way and save us.

115. Do not fall asleep forever. The Gospel of Christ is like an alarm clock. It tells you it is time to wake up or else perish.

116. We are given sight to see, but we do not see the light of Christ! We are so used to living in darkness that we have lost sight.

117. Dreaming is a rare gift to humans. Lucky are those who can dream; it helps them to escape the awful reality of this world.

118. People are often asked, "Are you a believer?" Those who commit the worst crimes against humanity under the banner of religion and in the name of God are believers. So, before answering,

pause for thought.

119. Righteousness is timeless and has passed the limits of this physical universe. However, the actions of the unrighteous have confined them to this mortal existence with no way out. Never envy their gains.

120. Jesus said, "The kingdom of heaven is like a mustard seed...." The mustard seed is the smallest of seeds. Do not feel belittled; you are the seed that will grow to great heights to please the Lord.

121. Pray and praise the Lord, give alms, and preach the gospel of Christ. We are Jesus's humble servants, and it is he who will harvest the field.

122. There are many secrets in this world. The greatest one is, " Who will inherit the kingdom of God?" Knock on Jesus's door. He will tell you what you will need to know, and it will astound you.

123. Serve Jesus Christ with humility and leave egotism behind for the dying world. Look what narcissism has done to humanity.

124. Jesus said, "Blessed are the poor, for theirs is the kingdom of God." (Like 6-20) Why did Jesus not say, "Blessed are the rich who give to the poor, for theirs is the kingdom of God"? Are worldly riches so bad?

A poetic reflection on life

Ah Love! Could you and I with Him conspire
To grasp this sorry Scheme of Things entire
Would not we shatter it to bits – and then
Re-mould it nearer to the Heart's Desire!

We are no other than a moving row
Of Magic Shadow-shapes that come and go
Round with the Sun-illuminated Lantern held
In Midnight by the Master of the show

I sent my Soul through the Invisible
Some letter of that After-life to spell
And by and by my Soul return'd to me
And answer'd "I Myself am Heav'n and Hell"

Oh threats of Hell and Hopes of Paradise!
One thing at least is certain – This life flies
One thing is certain and the rest is lies
The Flowers that once has blown for ever dies

With them the seed of wisdom did I sow
And with mine own hand wrought to make it grow
And this was all the Harvest that I reap'd
"I came like water, and like Wind I go."

Some for the Glories of This World;
and some Sigh for the Prophet's Paradise to come
Ah, take the Cash, and let the Credit go
Nor heed the rumble of a distant Drum

Before the phantom of False morning died
Methought a Voice within the Tavern cried
"When all the Temple is prepared within,
why nodes the drowsy Worshipper outside?"

Omar Khayyam

References

1. B. Layton. The Gnostic Scriptures. SCM Press Ltd, London, 1097. (ISBN:0-334-02022-0)

2. E. FitzGerald. Rubaiyat of Omar Khayyam. Second Edition, Eghbal Publications. 1986.

About the author

Dr Ali Ansarifar is a Persian-born retired British academic who has been living in the United Kingdom for 50 years. He was awarded a bachelor's degree and a doctorate in Materials Science from Queen Mary College, University of London, and a diploma in interface science from Imperial College, University of London. He worked as a postdoctoral research assistant at Imperial College London and the Cavendish Laboratory, Department of Physics, University of Cambridge. He was an upper-senior research scientist in a rubber research and development centre in Hertfordshire, UK, and a lecturer in polymer engineering in the Materials Department at Loughborough University until he retired as a senior lecturer.

He has given lectures, seminars, and workshops in the United States, the United Kingdom, Europe, the Middle East, and Southeast Asia. He has published over 150 books and technical research papers in peer-reviewed international scientific journals, conference papers, articles in technical magazines for the polymer and tyre industries and textbooks and contributed chapters to scientific books. He has been on the editorial boards of Rubber and Adhesion scientific journals and has been awarded prizes for his scientific publications. He is a Fellow of the Higher Education Academy, UK, and a servant of Jesus Christ.

About the book

The biblical narrative addresses God and his creation, humanity and the universe, and Jesus Christ and salvation. There are many views among Christians about what the biblical narrative means, and this subject is under constant scrutiny. In the toolbox of literary works, poems and poetic verses are probably the most effective means to communicate with others. They contain meaning, clarity, depth and simplicity.

The proverbs and poetic verses presented here express the learning and understanding of the poet from his long and exciting Christian journey. A reflection on different aspects of God's creation – the universe, humanity, and salvation in Christ – provides a more universal and a less formal platform on which Christians can share their faith. One never knows where reflection will take us.

A personal reflection

Duality of light and darkness – The creation of humankind had to happen to free light from destructive coexistence with darkness. God (light) was liberated in Jesus Christ when the cursed duality was dissolved, and a perfect unity was achieved. Somehow, the benefits have not yet quite reached us in this life to improve or eradicate suffering and predicaments. The Gospel of Christ bridges the gap between the present turmoil and the future kingdom of God to fulfil God's promises to the elect. Meanwhile, the faithful must share the beauty and promises of the Gospel of Christ with others. So, there is hope despite the gloom.

> Walk in the dark and strive along;
> ask Jesus, where is the light?
> I am blind and see no path;
> have mercy, show me the ark.
>
> Here I am, where are others?
> I see suffering, I see tears.
> Be brave, suffer the trials.
> For years have passed, where is the bride?
>
> I hate darkness, I hate senseless.
> I struggle to see meaning.
> All I see is tasteless.
> Where is the one who is boundless?

Be my eyes be my guide.
Do not abandon me to guilty eyes.
Light the way and save the day.
You are the light, I am the bay.

It is all like a circus.
Men go around in a circle.
God's mercy reaches some in the circus.
Jesus cries, oh men, get out of the circle.

Men have eyes and blindness.
Men have ears and deafness.
Deafness and blindness are useless.
Christ's light shines in fullness; blindness and deafness become hopeless.

It is wisdom not idiocy.
It is mercy not cruelty.
It is faith not fantasy.
It is God's mercy and Christ's humanity, not human vanity.

Keep going until reaching nowhere;
in nowhere, ask, where am I?
Destiny replies, you have turned the wrong way;
Turn the right way while you can. "It never is too late" said, "I AM He."

He is here, He is there, and He is everywhere.
Nowhere is nearer than here.
Stay here; He will find you.
He is the author of Here, There, and Everywhere.

Deny the truth if you will.
The universe is big, and He will find you.
Why did you run away? He will ask you.
I am your father, He will tell you.

Like our ancestors we deny God.
Like our ancestors we embrace the odds.
How odd we do not see God.
Despite all the odds, we are destined for God.

Hide wherever you like.
Go to the east, go to the west.
Go to the north, go to the south.
There is no hiding place other than God.
How odd we have east, west, north, and south!

Never have any fear.
Jesus is always near.
Remember those who departed and are no longer here;
they dwell in splendid places, for they are so dear.

Seek Jesus while he is still here.
Travel on a golden bridge to a distant land
that is so far away and yet so near.
The magic is waiting. Come, my dear.
Jesus is here. Why the fear?

Look around; what do you see?
Fear, anxiety, and senseless vanity.
Men are trapped in endless insanity.
What happened to our love of nobility?
Are we all lost to the curse of depravity?

Men are burdened with iniquities and alienation.
They need forgiveness and jubilation.
Jesus lightens the load and removes indignation.
Repentance frees a man from subjugation.

A man was walking along a road full of holes;
he felt rejected and laden with woes.
Jesus called; do not fall into the holes.
I am here to give you respite and hope.

Emancipation, reconciliation, purification, and salvation;
four notes in the melody of jubilation.
Jesus Christ is the jubilee's incarnation.
Church bells declare the faithful's sanctification.

I heard a voice from a distant land;
rejoice, oh men; God will soon light the land.
Angels, archangels, Jesus, and God's hand;
will welcome the elect to the promised land.

Strolling along a road in the promised land;
I saw a man who raised both hands.
I am the one who was shattered and without land;
I now have a mansion and beautiful land.

It was the first day in the kingdom of God;
men were dancing and singing for the glory of God.
Jesus uttered; "How happy I am to see you here in this land."
Men yelled, "Bless you Jesus for leading us to this holy land."

Walking along the river of eternal life;
a gentle soul crossed my line.
I asked, Have I not seen you in the former life?
Yes, it replied. "You preached to me Jesus Christ, the bread of life;
here I am, a new life."

Marvel at He who draws men near to Him.
Pure and noble are He.
Men's hearts and souls offer delightful hymns.
True faith, the source of wondrous myths.

Tears rolling, tears flowing.
Man's sorrow and heartbreak growing.
River of tears and river of mercy joining.
Jesus blesses the flows that are adjoining.

Jesus spoke to a man who was adoring.
Happiness and gratitude were overflowing.
Thank you, Lord, for your love;
so abundant and so luring.

The farmer and the field

Plant some seeds in a distant field.
Reap the crop and produce a yield.
Peel the yield from the weeds.
Place the yield into a weedless field.
Watch the yield growing into an endless heap.
Praise God, what an amazing scene.

The Kingdom of God

Ascending angels and attending archangels.
Rainbow colours and exotic lights.
Scent of perfumes and sense of calm.
Eternal life flowing from a river so divine.
Purified souls and redeemed lives.
Grateful hearts and joyful times.
Love precious and so abundant;
fulfilling desires of every heart.
Nations praising and God raising.
God, Jesus, and man revelling.
Eternity unfolding, forever men exulting.
All so inviting and so enchanting.
What an astonishing height.
It all sounds like the Lark Ascending.

Final remarks by the author

I converted to the Christian faith over forty years ago after reading the Bible. I did not imagine that I would write books on my faith and the incredible experience of learning about God and Jesus Christ. The knowledge that God's revelation in Christ gave me is so precious that I must share it with others. My faith has gone through various stages and is shaped to serve the Gospel of Christ. What the Lord God has given me I have put on paper, and I hope others will benefit from it as indeed I have done so from the writings of my fellow Christians over the years. It is all for the glory of God through our Lord Jesus Christ, and I am privileged to be called to serve him.

Books by the author

Sharing the Faith. Kingdom Publishers, London, UK. 2021.
ISBN: 978-1-913247-54-6

The Bible Story of Mankind. A Covenant with God with no Get-out Clause. Balboa Press, UK. 2021. ISBN: 978-1-9822-8394-0 (sc).
ISBN: 978-1-9822-8393-3 (e).

Why Did God Create Mankind? The Problem of Duality with God. Balboa Press, UK. 2021.
ISBN: 978-1-9822-8439-8 (sc). ISBN: 978-1-9822-8440-4 (e).

The British and American Empires and the State of Israel. Until the Kingdom of God Comes. Kingdom Publishers, London, UK. 2022.
ISBN: 978-1-913247-98-0

The March to the Armageddon, Balboa Press, UK 2022.
ISBN: 978-1-9822-8377-3 (sc), ISBN: 978-1-9822-8378-0 (e)

How Did God Create Mankind? Scientific and Biblical Views. Kingdom Publishers, London, UK. 2022.
ISBN: 978-1-911697-64-0

Why does Judaism reject Jesus Christ? Unintended Messianic expectations and unplanned temple-worship. Kingdom Publishers, London, UK. 2023.
ISBN: 978-1-911697-73-2

A Brief History of the World – The Great Deception. Kingdom Publishers, London, UK. 2024.
ISBN: 978-1-916801-01-1

The deep state and its agenda for humanity. Kingdom Publishers, London, UK. 2024.
ISBN: 978-1-916801-29-5

www.ingramcontent.com/pod-product-compliance
Lightning Source LLC
Chambersburg PA
CBHW061226070526
44584CB00029B/4001